Dancing with My Daughter

Other Loyola Press Books
by Jayne Jaudon Ferrer

A New Mother's Prayers
poems of love, wisdom & dreams

A Mother of Sons
poems of love, wisdom & dreams

Dancing with my Daughter

poems of love, wisdom & dreams

Jayne Jaudon Ferrer

LOYOLAPRESS.

CHICAGO

LoyolaPress.

3441 N. Ashland Avenue
Chicago, Illinois 60657
(800) 621-1008
www.loyolabooks.org

Cover illustration: Clifford Alejandro
Cover and interior design by Megan Duffy Rostan

Library of Congress Cataloging-in-Publication Data

Ferrer, Jayne Jaudon.
  Dancing with my daughter : poems of love, wisdom & dreams / Jayne
Jaudon Ferrer.
      p. cm.
  ISBN 0-8294-1768-0
  1. Mothers and daughters—Poetry. 2. Motherhood—Poetry. 3.
Women—Poetry. 4. Girls—Poetry. I. Title.
  PS3556.E72578D36 2004
  811'.54—dc22

                                        2003014828

Printed in the United States
  ·· 04 05 06 07 M-V 10 9 8 7 6 5 4 3 2·

For my mother,
who taught me to be fearless.

Contents

Acknowledgments

As I struggled to come up with an appropriate title for this book, it occurred to me that the mother-daughter relationship—with all its twists and turns, and ups and downs, and diversity and passion and drive—is very much like a dance. We come together—for celebration, support, or commiseration; we back away—in anger or confusion, for privacy or reflection. But in one form or another, the "dance" goes on throughout our lives; we simply vary the rhythm and who gets to lead when. With that image in mind, *Dancing with My Daughter* evolved into five sections: "Waltz," focusing on those early years when all is tender togetherness; "Jitterbug," which covers those lively toddler and childhood years; "Tango," for those breathless preadolescent days; "Samba," addressing that fiery teenage phase; and "Freestyle," which deals with the promises and dreams of the future.

I have so, so many people to thank for their role in helping this book come together—many of whom may not even realize they had a part in it. Specifically, though, I want to thank the following: Debbie Bass, Jane Counts, Dot Nichols, Margaret Rawson, and Lou Rogers for being loyal friends and very wise mothers of daughters; Michelle Brassel, Krystal McCloud, Katie and Summer Rawson, Rachel and Sarah Rogers, and Heather, Heidi, Hillary, and Hannah Wall for being brilliant and promising and sharing themselves with me; Gayle Bailey, Cheryl Bishop, Pam Black, Robbi Burts, Jane Comer, Sandra Jaudon, Elaine Lister, Carole and Jenna Lyles, Vivian Mirk, Eleanor Simmons, Beth Trane, Kathy Wall, Pat Yoder, and Patty Young for reflecting on memories and moments in their lives; Aubrey Curtis, Felts and Patsy Dent, Teri Gimmel, Joan Harmon, Emily Sue Harvey, Betty Jaudon, Margo LaGatutta,

Amy Markowich, Jon and Sue Martin, Ray and Kay Simmons, Dana Welch, and Barbara Wilson for helping to save the chocolate poem; and Mary Lou Carney, Kay Day, Jeanette Guinn, Glenis Redmond, and Dana Wildsmith for their love of words and for their kind endorsements.

A special thank you to my editor Joe Durepos, for changing careers and taking me with him, to Rebecca Johnson, for making what might have been drudgery into a genuinely satisfying experience, to Julie Nielsen for staying right on top of things, and to the entire production team at Loyola for their warm reception and strong support.

Sadly, the person who was the greatest inspiration to me when writing this book, my mother, will never know it, because she is now a victim of Alzheimer's disease. Amazingly, in the midst of the heartache this horrible malady inflicts, wonderful moments happen. As my mother relived her girlhood days, I was blessed to be able to experience those memories with her. Out of that came two things: the commitment to complete this book, and the realization that, even though the mother-daughter dance will eventually end, its steps are pressed into our hearts forever. I hope my words can be a conduit for appreciating yours anew.

Blessings,
J.J.F.

Waltz

*"Having a daughter has given me a reason
to reach higher and be more than I am."*

—Debbie, mother of Christy

Heirloom

I remember this dress!
It was my favorite.
I loved it because it was buttercup yellow,
because the fabric was softer than skin,
because the sunflower buttons made me smile,
because Mother made it
just for me.
Look at you wearing it now!
Wouldn't your grandmother be proud?
And shouldn't I be ashamed
that such superlative sewing skills
seem to have skipped a generation?
I can make you a cake, my darling.
I can make you a nursery rhyme.
But I cannot make you a
soft yellow dress with sunflower buttons.
And that is my loss,
much more than yours.

Portrait

Here we sit—
two girls—
surrounded by all things pink.
I look at your fingers
    so tiny!
kiss them,
caress them,
    wonder
what all will fall
within their grasp.

Your eyes are wide
and merry,
as though you know
some delectable secret
and can't wait until I
discover it, too.

But it is your skin
that captivates me.
So pure!

Fairly glistening
with unsullied newness of life.
My finger is a sponge
as I trace across your temple,
    tickle across your tummy,
        tease across your toes.
I soak up your
    virgin essence
like a parched stem
sucking up summer rain.

Gorged on your glorious goodness,
drunk on your luminous glow,
I giggle,
you hiccup,
we bask
as here we sit—
two girls—
and the day
    disappears.

A Rose Is a Rose Is a Ruby?

Welcome to my world, Alicia.
This is my daughter, Babette.
Come in for dinner, Cassandra.
Pick up your toys, Yvette.
So many months we've had
to choose the perfect name;
From A to Z, from Z to A,
then back to Z again.
How do I tell the future,
divine who my daughter will be?
What if I call her Abby
and she turns out an Annabel Lee?

If we give her an odd name like Seryn,
will she like it, or loathe us for life?
But if she is plain Jane or Mary,
won't that cause just as much strife?
I feared that my greatest dilemma
as a mother would be down the road—
some crisis like failing a math test,
or a boy, or hormone overload.
But here I am panting through labor
(not even a real mother yet!),
and already I'm totally baffled
by this daughter I've not even met!

Gift

There,
momentarily mute,
lies the fusion of
yin and yang.
His discipline,
my zest.
His raven curls,
my straight blonde mane.
Our ability to look beyond
burned dinners and botched apologies
culminated in this
eight-pound amalgamation
of love.

She who has just left God
gazes up with complacent candor
at we who have waited so fervently,
so impatiently,
so long.
Such a big void
for so tiny a soul to fill!
Our hearts latch on,
lay claim,
like greedy toddlers.

Passing the Torch

My best memory
is of chilly winter mornings
when my mother draped my school clothes
over the furnace.
Warm from the fire,
warm from the heartflush of knowing
I was indisputably,
irrefutably
loved,
I would slip on my clothes,
wolf down my waffles,
face my day
fed and fortified.
It was a fine, fine feeling,
one I want you to know.

Can it be achieved with a dryer and bagels?
I wonder.
Perhaps I shall make your best memory
one of long walks and leisurely listening.
You can tell me anything and I will
listen and laugh
or listen and cry
or listen and do nothing at all
except love you—
indisputably,
irrefutably,
infinitum.

Dream Weaver

One dreams of having a daughter
for many reasons—
some simple,
some sweet,
some silly.
I wanted you so I could share what's good
     about our world:
fat puppies and perfect peaches,
music and magnolias,
hummingbirds and harvest moons and hugs.
I wanted you so I could share what's good
     about growing up:

families sharing autumn picnics,
romping in the snow,
feeling safe, feeling proud, and feeling loved.
I wanted you so I could share what's good
    about being a girl:
frilly dresses and French braids,
whispering and secrets,
double dates and Nancy Drew and malls.
Here's to dreams coming true, my daughter!
(Yours, as well as mine.)

September Lullaby

Mommy can turn the TV off,
Mommy can hide your eyes.
But Mommy can't make it go away;
Mommy can only apologize.

Mommy can wrap you in her arms,
Mommy can let you cry.
But Mommy's not sure she can explain;
Mommy can only try.

Mommy can hold you close at night,
Mommy can help you cope.
But Mommy can't say it won't happen again;
Mommy can only hope.

Mommy can teach you not to hate,
Mommy can teach you fair play.
But Mommy can't promise peace on earth;
Mommy can only pray.

Jitterbug

You look into your daughters' faces and know what they're thinking because you remember what it was like to be their age.

—Margaret, mother of
Summer and Katie

Her Father's (and Mother's) Daughter

He wanted a football player.
I wanted a little doll.
He wanted a rough-and-tumble tough guy
to romp in the yard with a dog.
I wanted a satin-and-lace sweetheart
to share tea and crumpets in the afternoon.
And so, here you are:
a little doll who loves football,
a rascal of the first degree—
so precious wrapped up
in your pristine, beribboned gown as
you
and Rover
scarf down Oreos
and Milk-Bones
off my finest crystal platter.

A Mismatch
Made in Heaven

It is cruelly hilarious,
is it not,
that she whose face
has never met Maybelline,
whose fashion statement
is limited to three words—
Polo, Levi, Nike—
whose hair is simply
there
gave birth to Barbie?
She of the flaxen curls
and pastel pearls

("Want my bow *here*, Mommy!"
"Those socks don't match my dress!"),
the piccolo giggles,
preening wiggles,
rapt rolled eyes,
impassioned sighs . . .
One wonders:
does God make mistakes,
or does he just have a
divine sense
of humor?

Mother Magic

It is a Diamond Tiara Beautiful Princess Day.
Or so I thought.
But when the Beautiful Princess awakens,
her Royal Highness is in a royal huff.
The diamond tiara is hurled
with great vigor
into the Corner Where All Stupid Things Go.
Ah, well.
Methinks the princess protesteth too much,
but what do I,
lowly commoner,
know?
Ever the humble servant,
I scurry to make amends:
"Perchance the Evil Queen Hildegaard
    is here instead?"

I grab the Queenly Scepter-cum-baton
and gingerly
extend it.
Faster than Merlin might wave his wondrous wand,
the Queenly Scepter goes sailing
toward Stupid Corner exile.
Well, then. Perchance not.
I draw a breath
and muse
as the creature glowers.
"It seems some vile and loathsome toad
has cast a spell on you, Princess."
(I pronounce this news in my most annoyed voice—
which requires hardly a modicum of effort.)
"Therefore you must be quarantined indefinitely!
I shall call your royal friends and explain that,

alas! the Princess may not play today."
In a moment of instant healing that would dazzle
the Lord himself,
Her Royal Highness experiences miraculous
    recovery.
"I broke the spell!" she shrieks, leaping
    from her throne,
"because I am a Princess and I can do anything!"
Well, well.
I am a mother,
and I can, too.

Turnaround

I think today is an ice cream day;
I'm pretty sure it is.
A day for sundaes, splits, or floats,
for sprinkles and extra fizz.
I think today was a big ol' mess;
I'm pretty sure it was.
A waste of everybody's time,
a bona fide lost cause.
I think today can turn around;
I'm pretty sure it will.
Mix you, and me, and ice cream—
things just have to head uphill!
I think today is turning out fine;
I'm pretty sure it has.
Aren't you glad that we have ice cream,
each other, and all that jazz?

Choosing Sides

The world is not simple now.
It was, once—
so they say.
You chose
skinning hides or
weaving baskets,
stitching samplers or
traveling abroad,
wrapping bandages or
bandaging scrapes.
Now we have many choices.
I do.
You do.
But no one should choose *for* you.
Because you may *want* to
skin hides or
weave baskets or
stitch linens or

see the world or
soothe the sick or
comfort babes.
Or
you *may* want to
fly jets or
flex pecs or
finance cars or
fill cavities or
frisk crooks or
fight injustice.
Our world is not simple now;
but it is
satisfying.
And I am glad your choice will derive from
genius
instead of gender.

Slumber Party

I know before you ask.
You have that look on your face.
That "Ohpleaseit'llbesomuchfun!"
"Ipromisewewon'tstayupallnight!"
look.
Yes, it will, of course,
and yes, you will, of course, but,
of course,
we'll have it anyway.
Lack of sleep is somehow
central
to growing up,
right in there with
playing dress up

and giggling
and giving tea parties.
There is something cathartic
about slumber parties.
Slightly wicked,
slightly silly,
(okay, supremely silly),
slightly elegant,
slightly mysterious . . .
a crash course in Womanhood 101.
Bring on the board games,
the blusher, and the brownies,
and let the big night begin!

Sidelines Perspective

"Way to watch!"
"Way to run!"
"Way to smack that ball!"
We fill the bleachers with our pride,
our cheers,
our fears.
"It's okay, honey!"
"Shake it off!"
"Next time!"
In the field,
you are intense,
oblivious.
Chin steeled in determination,
eyes squinted against the sun,
you want it—
but it's just a game.
To us, up there in the stands,
it's
so much
more.

Tango

Having a daughter is a million blessings and curses in one (small or large!) body. It's a constant roller coaster ride of emotions for both of us—pure joy, pure hatred (it's true!), pure delight, pure disgust, hysteria (both comic and tragic), frustration, amazement, and enormous fun. Sounds like the perfect definition of true love!

—Deryn, mother of Charlotte,
Madeleine, and Sophie

The Path Already Taken

I know that today
you hate me.
Hate me because,
this time,
I am right
and you are wrong.
But there will be other times.
I will not always be right.
Right is not a byproduct of
paychecks or Premarin or
pension funds.
My odds are better only
because I've been in your shoes
before.
(Were they this . . . umm . . .
clunky then?)

Budding Beauty

I catch you
trying on my bra.
Like a doe made immobile by
the glare of headlights,
you stand frozen in my stare—
a sight at once
lurid and adorable.
(A definite Kodak moment,
though I wouldn't dare.)
Taking in
the tangled heap of lace
on the bed before you,
the tubes and compacts

splayed on the counter behind you,
and the pitiful picture of your sweet lips
smeared
with "Cinnamon Sin" and "Mango Mama,"
(You're mixing colors? That's great!)
by a hand whose pudgy contours
will still grip lollipops better than lipstick
for some years to come,
I suppress my smile
and give an apprizing nod.
"Good choice.
Beige doesn't show through."

Loaded Question

"Mama, am I pretty?"

"You talking to me?
Are *you* talking to *me*?
Pretty? Why, darling, you're *beautiful!*
That soft, shiny hair . . .
that lovely, clear complexion . . .
that innocent smile . . . "

"No, Mama, I mean,
will *boys* think I'm pretty?
It doesn't matter what *you* think.
I mean, well . . . "

"Yeah, you *mean* well,
but, after all, I'm just a mom, right?
Chopped liver in pantyhose . . .
transportation with an attitude . . .
a wallet with a uterus . . . "

"MOM!"

"Okay, okay, fine.
Yes, my darling,
boys will think you're pretty.
Boys will be falling all over their
zitty little noses and
big stinky feet
for the merest glimpse of your
glorious countenance.
They'll come in hordes.
I'll have to beat them away at the door.
And the first one who touches you
will find the full fury of my fist
flattened firmly against his florid,
    fuzz-encrusted face . . . "

"MOM!"

"Sorry.
Yes, sweetie,
you're pretty."

Crush

Believe it or not,
I know how it feels.
For me,
it was Gary Stephens.
6'6", probably all of
130 pounds . . .
I thought he was gorgeous.
I timed all my locker breaks around his.
He didn't know I was alive.
So I know how it feels,
sweetheart.
When he doesn't smile back,
when he winks at someone else,
when you think, *"This* will be the day!",
but it isn't.

Today, that boy will not tease you
in the hallway.
Today, that boy will not ask you to
meet him at the mall.
Today that boy will not notice that
you are amazing, and can talk about anything,
and have incredible eyes.
But someday,
some boy
will.

The Crucible

I don't think you'll want to listen
when I tell you this will pass,
but it will.
I promise.
Right now, you hate her
    for knowing all your secrets
    for having half your stuff
    for liking the same clothes and CDs you do
    for being funny and cute and
        afraid of the soccer ball
    for all the things you loved about her
yesterday.
This is not the end of a friendship;
this is a test.
We girls do our testing with words and stares,
instead of sticks and stones.
Viciously virulent words.
White-hot withering stares.

Bloodless assaults that rip our victims apart
as brutally as any machete.
Don't wait till the wounds are infected.
Start heading for healing now.
Shut your mouth.
Shut your eyes.
Get some sleep.
Get some space.
Find an issue that's bigger than this.
(And most are.)
In a month, you'll hardly remember.
In a year, you may even laugh.
If not? Then it wasn't a friendship
meant to be,
and you can move on.

Ode to a Young Girl's Metamorphosis

It's what they call "the awkward stage"—
that purgatory before hormones rage,
when everything's sprouting except self-esteem,
(which is hurtling downhill with a
    full head of steam).
Your hair's stupid, you say; you feel weird in
    your clothes.
You're too old for socks; you're too young for hose.
If only your body could spin a cocoon—
a safe place to hide till you feel more in tune
with all of the havoc that Nature hath wrought.
(And emerging a beauty? Now *there's* a nice thought!)

The best news I have is that when this has passed,
you'll stop seeing yourself as a social outcast
and rise like a phoenix from hormonal ashes
to straighten your shoulders and flutter your lashes.
The new you will light up your old mise-en-scène
like bright morning sun lights up cold, dreary dawn.
So be patient, my dear! It won't be very long
till the "you" you don't like gets to sing her

    swan song.

The Sins of the Mother

Come, darling.
Let me speak to you of
chocolate.
Roll these words on your tongue:
Godiva, Ghirardelli, Perugina, Lindt,
Cadbury, Scharffen Berger, Dove.
These are the names you can turn to
when life overwhelms,
when men disappoint,
when friends forsake,
when you fail a test,
when you gain five pounds,
when your world falls apart,
when things fail to go according to plan.
What else, I ask,
can lower your cholesterol,
reduce your chance of a heart attack,

boost your endorphins,
flood you with antioxidants,
max you out on magnesium,
stir up your seratonin,
make you feel euphorically happy,
passionately loved,
and unequivocally, consummately
blessed?
Nothing other than
pure vanilla-laced,
70+ percent cocoa solids,
not too sweet,
but ohhhh so rich and
rapturous
chocolate.
(Let's have some, shall we?)

Samba

*On those occasions when my sisters and I found
ourselves lying to our mother, Mom would say
calmly, without any harsh acknowledgement,
"Beware! Your sins will find you out." She knew
from the beginning we were up to no good and
that she would find out the truth eventually!*

—Patty, daughter of Doris

Mom's Top Ten Tickets to Trouble

I'll be the first to admit it.
I have this thing about public spectacles.
It falls into my "a time and place
    for all things" obsession.
And while it's true that I have, on rare occasion,
fallen from grace (please, God,
    let no one remember!),
I intend that *you* shall not.
To wit:

1. We do not drape ourselves over our
    boyfriends in public. (We do not do it in
    private, either, but that's entirely another
    discussion.)

2. We do not pull up to red lights with our car
    windows down and our music blasting.
    (Exception: if you are listening to a
    particularly splendid concerto on NPR, or
    have borrowed my Vivaldi CD, you have my

permission to play dueling speakers with the Rap King beside you. You will lose, but at least you will have momentarily enriched the lives of those around you.)

3. If we are check-out clerks, we do not ignore and/or annoy our customers by discussing our latest crush or our plans for the weekend hence with the clerk two registers down.

4. We do not wear shirts that intentionally reveal our bra straps.

5. We do not wear cleavage to church.

6. We do not flaunt our navels as if they were hood ornaments.

7. We do not, in general, wear clothing that causes middle-aged men to endanger the lives of those around them by diverting their attention away from the operation of their automobiles and toward our figurative assets.

8. We do not engage in the hurling of French

fries, popcorn, small candies, or other foodstuffs across the theater/restaurant/mall in an effort to attract someone's attention.

9. We do not engage in inappropriate communal screaming, whooping, or woofing (ball games, rock concerts, and the Second Coming being obvious exceptions).

10. We do not leap into the street, convulse our bodies, beat on windows, or throw ourselves on car hoods in an effort to recruit potential customers for car washes, donut sales, or other fund-raising events.

You think my stance is harsh? You say nobody
    else's mother cares?
Well, dear, *somebody's* mother has to,
and I volunteer.

Prom

It is wicked of me, I know,
but as we look at
this dress
and then
that one,
then this one,
then that one,
little mouse voices keep creeping
in my brain,
echoing in my ear,
sneaking out my mouth:
"Cinderelly, Cinderelly,
gotta help our Cinderelly!"

Four weeks,
fourteen stores,
and a forty-hour paycheck later,
the quest is over.
Indeed,
you look as though a
fairy godmother just dusted you with
starlight.
Eyes shimmering with excitement,
cheeks rouged by adrenaline rush,
hair lustrous with the glow of anticipation . . .
Tonight,
you are not my daughter.
You are a dream.

Trial by Tryout

It's over by now;
you're either in or you're
not.
And still,
I don't know which way my heart is
leaning.
"In" is parties
and phone calls
and belonging
and memories.
"In" is also
pressure and pettiness
and jealousy and exclusion.

"Out" hurts
for a while,
sometimes forever,
but "out" can pave the way for
fresh ideas and first adventures,
opportunities that make being
"one of the gang"
look positively
mundane.
I've been in both places;
you will be, too.
But which will it be today?

Table Talk

Dear Daughter,

I'm writing this note because

☐ a) you are not talking to me this week

☐ b) there is a telephone in one ear and an
earphone in the other

☐ c) what with the purple hair and the silver
stud stuck through your eyebrow (please
tell me it's glued), I'm not sure it's really
you under the blanket on the couch.

We are having company tonight. When you come
home from school, please

☐ a) erase any overly passionate messages your
admirers may have left on the answering
machine

☐ b) set the table with the good dishes (the
Lenox, dear, not the Chinet)

☐ c) take down the poster you put up in the
kitchen (you know, the one that has
"Murderers!" scrawled over the heads of
Colonel Sanders and Ronald McDonald).

And, if you don't mind, I'd especially like it
tonight if you'd
☐ a) resist the urge to roll your eyes when Aunt
Bess asks for diet cola with her cheesecake
☐ b) skip the bit where you point to the
aquarium and ask if anyone wants sushi
☐ c) refrain from referring to my standing rib
roast as "carrion."

Looking forward to a pleasant evening,

Mom
P.S. Cooperate and I'll let you put kelp in the
broccoli soufflé!

Mellow Cello

I sit
superfluous, intrusive, with
assorted other in-the-way parents.
We are on *your* turf,
along only for the ride
you needed to get here today.
Scanning the cafeteria-cum-warm-up-room,
I see
a great deal more artifice than artistry.
Most do not want to be here, I think.
They are sucking up to Grandma
or weaseling out of math.
But amid the acute cacophony,
I watch
some who feel the music,
some who hear the passion.
One of those is you.
I stare
embarrassed and enchanted
as you caress your imposing instrument

like a needy lover,
nestling against its slender neck,
palming its umber curves, your bow
undulating across the bridge of strings
like fingertips dancing on fire.
I sigh
knowing you do not need me here,
do not need me in many spaces
of your life anymore.
And, so, when they call out your name,
I thrill
to see the subliminal staccato
"Mayday!" that leaps from your eyes
to mine, and
I beam
at you, and validate us
both.
You will make it, my darling—
if not today, most assuredly,
in life.

DNA Denouement

If my mother is a rose,
then I am a poppy.
She, dignified, resilient,
dependable.
I, carefree, capricious,
more likely to flourish
in an open field
than a tended bed.
We are both red—
though she more vibrant than I—
my bright petals no match for
that vermilion charm that oozes,
even now, through age and infirmity
like blood through gauze.

Still, her thorns have
pricked more than a few.
My stems are tender;
I bruise and wilt
when the world comes
shoving past.

I love
my mother's smooth, olive skin,
her waves of silver hair,
her green thumb that might be
God's own.

She loathes
my manic schedule,
my paper scraps and untidy piles,
my as-often-as-possible bare feet—
trademark traits for years.

We are neither opposites
nor two of a kind,
not best friends, mortal enemies,
inseparable, or estranged.
We are women who share
a gene pool,
a fondness for flowers,
a propensity for pouting,

who have lived through the loss of
a good man,
the abuse of
a bad one,
polar hormonal onslaughts,
the best of times,
the worst of times,
who have now reversed roles,
slapped death in the face
(several times),
and emerged
friends.

Domesticity Specificity

When I said "Clean up your room!" last night,
what do you suppose I might have meant?
Close the door so I couldn't see the clutter?
No.
Kick the clothes and shoes and the—
decoupaged bowling balls?
—under the bed?
Noooo.
Spray Febreze with great abandon so that
periodically
there is a whiff of something not *quite* so profane
as month-old pizza and mildewing towels?
No, no, and, most emphatically, *no*.
What I meant,
oh, dearest darling, fair-faced fruit of my womb,
precious child for whom I labored long and hard

(and was happy to do so!),
is that you are to disconnect—
at this precise moment—
all electronic appendages
from your person,
fit your dainty hand
around a rag and a can of cleanser,
fill your ears with the mighty music of the
    vacuum cleaner,
your lungs with the derelict dust of this
    dreadful domain,
and *dig in, sister!*
(I'll just hold all your calls till you're done.)

Freestyle

*Because of my mother's support and
belief in my dreams, I believe I can be
anything or do anything I want.*

—Kara, daughter of Elaine

Red Riding Hood Revisited

All the things my grandmother was not,
I will be for your daughter.
I will tease her with sprigs of dandelion
in the springtime,
tempt her with ripe red melons
in the summer sun,
laugh with her in the languid blaze
of autumn,
cherish her warmth in the starkness
of winter's chill.
We will have secrets,
she and I.
About cookies
and boyfriends,
lipsticks
and lollipops,
late nights,

early mornings,
and love.
I will wipe away her freckles
with the milky mist of twilight;
she will wipe away my age spots
with the dew.
Together, we will
fret about,
forage through, and
feast upon life
from
one end
to the other.

Aftermath

Fine.
You hate me.
I love you anyway.
But guess what?
I don't like you
sometimes.
You're messy,
you're rude, and well,
look at you!
You're young and
fresh and
beautiful . . .
and I am,
well,
not.

But even when I'm mad at you
I think you're smart
and funny
and creative
and kind,
and despite
that room
and those glares
and the fact that my
favorite shirt will
always look better on you,
I'm still glad
to be your mother.

Send-off

I have only two requests:
come home without holes
in your body
(beyond those given you by God),
and keep in mind
that old saying about
nice girls
and newspaper headlines—
you know, weddings
and funerals
and Nobel Prizes
only.
(That last one is mine—
I would never want to stifle you.)
The rest, my dear, is up to
you,
'cause if I haven't taught it by now,
it won't sink in
tonight.

You go
with my blessing,
my encouragement,
my respect,
my love,
and my MasterCard.
I
will pray for us
both.

All in Favor, Say Nay

This could be the one,
and I approve—
wholeheartedly.
But I'd die before I'd tell you.
Last time,
you dropped that dear, sweet
dental student
like he was used floss
in a puddle of pond scum.
His hands in all those mouths
grossed you out, you said.
There are worse professions,
believe me.
I just thank the Lord
He led you on past that
bluegrass banjo picker.
Really!

I did not raise my daughter
for a life of boogie-down,
backwoods barn fests!
But this boy,
he has potential.
Good haircut, good job,
eats asparagus, appreciates art,
and has no tattoos (that I can see).
What more could a mother-in-law
ask for?

Veiled Retrospective

I have one piece of advice.
Okay, well, two.
Possibly three.
The point is,
do it the way *you* want to.
Twenty years after the fact,
I'm still wondering how
that saleswoman talked me into
lime chiffon sheaths for my
bridesmaids.
Or why I settled for mums
when I wanted
magnolias.
There aren't many chances in life
when you get to call all the shots.
So carpe diem, my darling!
Make the memories perfect,
make the day your own,
make the moments magic enough
to last a lifetime long.

Essential Minutia

There are certain bits of knowledge
that a woman must possess—
random tips and sundry tidbits
that I feel I must address.
So, in no specific order,
I've prepared for you this list.
(Keep it handy, dear, in case there are
some things I might have missed.)

One should always have a tissue.
One should always have clean feet.
One need not spend lots on clothing,
but one always must be neat.

Promptly send your thank-you notes.
Promptly pay your bills.
Promptly flush and wash your hands.
Promptly wipe up spills.

Get your oil changed faithfully.
Don't play with your hair.
Don't talk if food is in your mouth.
Be sure to pay your share.

If you get an invitation
that is marked "R.S.V.P.",
Make *certain* you respond!
(Yes, *this* one is my pet peeve!)

And should you start to wonder
if these rules fit current trends,
remember: it is *Mom's* advice
on which one must depend!

Homage

Virginia Woolf once said
we all need a room of our own.
Perhaps not a room but,
    most definitely,
        a place—
"where neither moth nor rust doth corrupt,
where thieves do not break through nor steal."
A heaven on earth,
    if you will—
        a revitalizing place to retreat
            when frustration and fatigue
            close in like hungry vultures,
someplace where there isn't any trouble,
someplace where your heart is nourished,
someplace where your soul is fed,
        someplace that feels like Home.

My place is
    my mother's back porch, at dusk—
        mist nuzzling the brown cows
        in the pasture sprawled green and lush
at the foot of a mountain . . .
        tree frogs singing rounds with cicadas,
        their vibrating chorus
an aural yin and yang account of
        events of the day.
And as the last pink streaks of sky ebb to gray,
    the firefly light show commences—
        yellow polka-dots flashing lazily
        like coy lanterns
            dancing in the darkening stillness.

Find your retreat, my darling,
    that place of escape and
      assured restoration
    that will set you free,
      make you whole,
        take you home.
We mothers worry about so many things—
    are you safe? are you satisfied?
    are you happy? are you loved?—
but we worry less if we know
    that wherever life leads,
    whatever it brings,
there's a place you call Home
    in your heart.

About the Author

Jayne Jaudon Ferrer speaks frequently to women's groups, writers' groups, schools, and civic organizations. If you're interested in scheduling a reading, presentation, or workshop, please visit her website at www.jaynejaudonferrer.com.